The Princess
and the Pea

Retold by Susanna Davidson

Illustrated by
Mike Gordon

Reading Consultant: Alison Kelly
University of Surrey Roehampton

Contents

Chapter 1

The picky prince

Once upon a time there was a prince who wanted to marry a princess. But he didn't want just any old princess. He wanted a *real* one.

This is Princess Cordelia, Your Highness.

Not one of the local princesses would do.

"What's the matter with them, Patrick?" cried his father, the king. "I'm running out of princesses to show you."

Are they too old? Too tall? Too hairy?

"I can't be sure they're real," sighed Prince Patrick. "I'll have to find one for myself."

"You must do whatever you want, darling," said the queen, who spoiled him rotten.

The next day Prince Patrick set out to travel the world, in search of a real princess.

He took with him twelve suitcases, ten pairs of shoes, a spare crown and his cousin, Fred.

"Goodbye, my love," cried the queen, wiping away a tear with her silk handkerchief.

They hadn't gone far when
they heard a loud sneeze from
under the seat.

"Who's there?" shouted
the prince.

A small figure crept out.

It's Peg!

"Aren't you the palace
maid?" said Prince Patrick.

Peg nodded.

"Well, what are you doing here?" the prince asked.

"I want to see the world," said Peg. "I've been at the palace all my life – ever since I was left on the doorstep as a baby."

I want an adventure!

She blushed. "And Cook's furious because I burned the pudding," she added.

"Well you can't come with us," said Fred. "This is a boys-only adventure."

"We're not turning back now," said Prince Patrick. "She'll have to join us."

10

Peg grinned at Fred.

"OK," Prince Patrick went on. "First stop, the wicked witch's hut."

Fred looked alarmed. "You are joking?"

She'll eat us alive!

Who's scared now?

Prince Patrick shook his head. "The witch will know how to find a real princess. She's my best hope..."

Chapter 2

Off to see the witch

"Now Peg," said Prince
Patrick, "this could be
dangerous. You stay in the
coach. Fred and I will meet
the witch."

The prince knocked three
times on the witch's door...
There was no answer.

Why couldn't
I stay in the
coach?

"Looks like no one's in. We'll
have to go," said Fred, who
was already backing away.

13

"She must be in," said the
prince, and he bent down to
peer through the keyhole.

A large green eye was staring
at him. Prince Patrick jumped
back and landed bottom-first
in a patch of mud.

14

A short plump woman opened the door, chuckling to herself. "Did I scare you? I was just checking who you were. You can't be too careful these days."

Look at this mud!

Fred was amazed. "Are you the witch?" he asked. "You're not scary at all."

The witch looked rather upset. "I try my best," she sighed. "I grew three new warts last week."

"Come inside," she added.
"I'm just cooking some tasty
soup for lunch."

Subthig really sbells in here.

I think it's the soup.

"We're not hungry," said
Prince Patrick quickly. "I've
come to ask for your help. I
want to know how to find a
real princess."

"Real princesses are very rare," said the witch, "and it's hard to spot a fake one. But there is a test you can do."

Let me see...

"A real princess must have... boiled brains, rotten beans and cat spit."

"What?" cried the prince.

"Oh sorry, that's a recipe for soup. This is it..."

17

The real princess test

A real princess must possess ...

1. Politeness to one and all

2. Kindness to rich and poor

3. Very sensitive skin

"Sensitive skin?" Prince Patrick asked, looking confused.

"A real princess," explained the witch, "has such tender skin that she could feel a pea under twenty mattresses."

"Thank you," said the prince. "You've been very helpful." He turned to the door.

"Oh do stay for lunch," pleaded the witch. "My soup's almost ready."

They were stuck in the witch's hut until the cauldron was empty.

"I feel sick," groaned Peg on the way back to the coach.

"Well, you shouldn't have had three bowls then," said Fred.

I poured mine into a plant pot.

"I was being polite! I didn't want to hurt the witch's feelings."

"That was very kind of you, Peg," said Prince Patrick, smiling at her.

"Where are we going now?" asked Fred.

"Now I have the witch's test, I can finally find a real princess," said the prince. "We're off to meet Princess Prunella. Check the map, Fred."

Princess Map

N
W   E
S

Princess Prudence

Princess Prunella

Princess Primrose

Princess Pavlova

Chapter 3

Princess Prunella

Princess Prunella was very excited to see the prince.

"You must come and stay in my castle," she cried.

She raced over the bridge, dragging Prince Patrick with her. "Hurry! Hurry!" she called to her servants.

He's perfect. We'll be married in no time.

"I want you to prepare the best bedchambers for the prince and Fred."

"Excuse me," said Peg,
struggling with all the luggage.
"Where am I to sleep?"

"Maids belong in the attic,"
replied the princess, haughtily.
"There might be a few mice
there, but I'm sure you'll cope."

24

Peg went to her room. It was cold and damp. She could hear mice scuttling about, squeaking.

Meanwhile, Fred and the prince were in the grand dining room with Princess Prunella.

"You're being very kind," said Prince Patrick, "but what about Peg? Is she eating in the kitchen?"

The princess looked shocked. "Your beastly little maid? You can't expect *me* to bother with *her.*"

She can eat the pig slops if she's hungry.

"I'm afraid we must leave," said Prince Patrick. "You're not a real princess after all."

26

"Oh yes I am!" cried Princess Prunella.

"Oh no you're not!" shouted Fred. "You've failed the first real princess test."

Rats!

"Real princesses are polite to everyone," explained Prince Patrick, "and you've just been rude to Peg."

27

Chapter 4

Princess Pavlova

"I won't give up!" said Prince Patrick. "There must be a real princess somewhere..."

"According to this map, there's a Princess Pavlova next door. Let's try her," Fred suggested.

28

Princess Pavlova greeted them all very politely.

"What a pleasure to have you here," she said. "Welcome to my castle."

Thank you, Your Highness.

"She's passed the politeness test," thought the prince. "Now what's the next one..."

Hmm. I have an idea.

2. Kindness to rich and poor

"Fred!" he cried, "I have a plan. I'm going to dress up as a beggar and see if Princess Pavlova is kind to me."

"Try out your disguise on Peg first," said Fred, "to make sure it works."

Prince Patrick found Peg sitting on a tree stump, about to eat an apple.

I'm a hungry beggar. Have you any food for me?

"Oh you poor thing!" Peg cried, when she saw him. "Here, have my apple."

Prince Patrick was very pleased with himself. "Excellent! It works," he shouted, throwing off his disguise.

It's you!

"What are you doing?" asked Peg. But the prince was already knocking on the castle door, to try the test on Princess Pavlova.

A servant answered.

"Is someone there?" called Princess Pavlova.

"It's a beggar, Your Highness."

"We've got nothing for him," snapped the princess. "Tell him to go away."

And he smells.

Prince Patrick turned away. "She's not a real princess," he thought. "A real princess is both polite *and* kind – even to beggars."

Chapter 5

A real princess

I'll never be married.

"I give up," said the prince, with a sigh. "I don't think there's a real princess anywhere. We may as well go home."

They got ready for the long
journey back to the palace.
Everyone was glum, even
the horses.

I bet Cook hasn't
forgotten about the
pudding I burned.

The coach arrived at the
palace just in time. A huge
storm was brewing.

Peg was sent straight
to the kitchens in disgrace.
"You've got hundreds of
dishes to wash," scolded
the cook. "They've
been piling up since
you left."

Prince Patrick and Fred went
to find the king and queen.
Outside, rain began beating
against the windows. Streaks
of lightning lit up the sky.

Just then, there was a knock on the door.

"There is a Princess Primrose to see you, Your Highness," said the footman.

Not another one!

A beautiful princess stepped into the room. She was wet from the rain and shaking with cold.

"I'm so sorry to trouble you," she said politely, "but my coach has broken down."

"No trouble at all," said Prince Patrick quickly. "Why don't you stay the night at our castle? We'll fix your coach in the morning."

Thank you! I must give you something in return.

"She acts like a real princess," thought the prince, "but I must be sure."

3. Very sensitive skin

He asked the servants to prepare Princess Primrose's bedroom.

"I want twenty mattresses on the bed," ordered Prince Patrick, "and a pea at the very bottom."

Here's your bed, Your Highness.

It's rather high...

Peg didn't get to bed that night. She had to finish washing the dishes.

The next morning, Princess Primrose came down for breakfast, looking refreshed.

"How did you sleep?" asked Prince Patrick.

I slept like a baby.

"I loved all those mattresses," the princess said. "It was the most comfortable bed."

Prince Patrick sighed. "A real princess would have felt that pea," he thought. He waved goodbye to Princess Primrose as soon as breakfast was over.

Another fake one!

She's not good enough for my Patrick.

It was Peg's job to clean the princess's bedroom. Slowly, she climbed up the ladder, yawning with each step.

"I'll just lie down for a moment," Peg thought, "before I start cleaning up."

Zzzzzzz

In no time at all, she was fast asleep.

An hour later, Peg woke
with a start.

"Ow!" she said. "There's
something really lumpy in this
bed. I'm getting down."

Ooh. It's a long
way.

But as she leaned over, she
knocked the ladder. It clattered
to the ground.

"Drat!" Peg cried. "I'm stuck."

"Help!" she shouted, as loudly as she could, "I'm stuck. Please... HELP!"

Everyone rushed into the bedroom.

"What are you doing up there?" Prince Patrick called.

"I was supposed to be cleaning," said Peg, "but I was so tired I fell asleep."

"And there's something horribly hard in this bed," she added. "I'm covered in bruises."

This can only mean one thing.

"I can't believe it!" cried the prince. "You were polite to the witch, kind to a beggar and now you've felt a pea under twenty mattresses. *You* must be a real princess!"

He raced up the ladder. "Peg, will you marry me?"

Peg gasped. "You want to marry *me*, a palace maid? Yes please!"

A maid?

But a princess at heart!

"Three cheers for Princess Peg," shouted Fred, and everyone cheered.

46

So Prince Patrick finally married his real princess. He put the pea in a glass case in the palace museum for everyone to see.

It may still be there today...

The Princess and the Pea was first told by Hans Christian Andersen. He was born in Denmark in 1805, the son of a poor shoemaker. He left home at fourteen to seek his fortune and became famous all over the world as a writer of fairy tales.

Series editor: Lesley Sims

Designed by Russell Punter
and Natacha Goransky

Digital illustration by Carl Gordon

First published in 2004 by Usborne Publishing Ltd., Usborne House, 83-85 Saffron Hill, London EC1N 8RT, England. www.usborne.com
Copyright © 2004 Usborne Publishing Ltd.